Writing 1

CAMBRIDGE SKILLS FOR FLUENCY

Cambridge Skills for Fluency is a series of supplementary materials covering the skills of listening, speaking, reading and writing; each skill is developed at four levels, from pre-intermediate through to advanced.

The series aims to develop students' confidence and fluency in English, by offering a variety of topics and activities which engage students' interest and encourage them to share their personal reactions and opinions.

Although all the books in the series share the same underlying principles, we have tried to avoid complete uniformity across the series, and so each book has its own features and its own particular approach to skills development:
- The *Listening* books aim to develop students' ability to understand real-life spoken English, through recordings of natural, spontaneous speech, selected and edited to make them accessible at each level.
- The *Speaking* books aim to develop oral fluency by focusing on topics that are personally relevant to students and which encourage students to draw on their own life experience, feelings and cultural knowledge.
- The *Reading* books aim to develop students' skill in reading English by introducing them to a wide variety of authentic texts, supported by tasks and activities designed to increase involvement and confidence in the reading process.
- The *Writing* books place writing in a central position in the language class, presenting it as a creative activity which contributes to language learning in general.

Level 1 of the series consists of the following titles:
Listening 1 by Adrian Doff and Carolyn Becket
Speaking 1 by Joanne Collie and Stephen Slater
Reading 1 by Simon Greenall and Diana Pye
Writing 1 by Andrew Littlejohn

CAMBRIDGE SKILLS FOR FLUENCY
Series Editor: Adrian Doff

Writing 1

Andrew Littlejohn

CAMBRIDGE
UNIVERSITY PRESS

PUBLISHED BY THE PRESS SYNDICATE OF THE UNIVERSITY OF CAMBRIDGE
The Pitt Building, Trumpington Street, Cambridge, United Kingdom

CAMBRIDGE UNIVERSITY PRESS
The Edinburgh Building, Cambridge CB2 2RU, UK
40 West 20th Street, New York, NY 10011–4211, USA
477 Williamstown Road, Port Melbourne, VIC 3207, Australia
Ruiz de Alarcón 13, 28014 Madrid, Spain
Dock House, The Waterfront, Cape Town 8001, South Africa

http://www.cambridge.org

First published 1991
Ninth printing 2002
Tenth printing 2003

Printed in the United Kingdom at the University Press, Cambridge

A catalogue record for this book is available from the British Library

ISBN 0 521 367565

GO

Contents

Map of the book

Unit	Aspects of writing	Structures	Functions	Vocabulary areas
1 Home sweet home	Labelling; lists; sentences.	There is/are; should; -ing form.	Expressing likes and dislikes.	Home routines; rooms.
2 Around the world	Labelling; notes.	Present simple.	Describing.	Countries; languages; geographical features.
3 Personal descriptions	Notes; grids; sentences.	Adjectives; very/quite; neither/nor.	Describing; expressing opinions and facts; giving reasons.	Adjectives.
4 DOs and DON'Ts	Notices; sentences.	Imperatives; present simple.	Stating rules; giving instructions; advising.	Social customs.
5 Expectations	Sentences; paragraphs.	Present simple; should; have.	Obligations; describing.	Jobs; objects.
6 Help yourself!	Lists; devising practice exercises.	Present tenses; past simple; imperatives; adjectives.	Social situations.	Learning English.
7 Business letters (1)	Business letters; letter layout.		Opening/closing; requesting; referring; enclosing.	Business letter conventions.
8 On the road	Explaining signs; writing directions.	Present simple; must.	Giving orders; warning; giving directions.	Road signs; travel; travel problems.
9 Forms	Completing forms.		Giving information.	Terms on forms.
10 Family life	Family trees; sentences.	Present tenses; have to.	Giving information; describing people; expressing opinions.	Family relationships.

Unit	Aspects of writing	Structures	Functions	Vocabulary areas
11 Business letters (2)	Business letters.		Apologising; complaining; giving good/bad news; giving reasons.	Business correspondence.
12 Jobs	Notes; sentences; paragraphs.	Present simple; have to.	Describing; giving reasons.	Jobs; personal qualities; action verbs.
13 DROW SELZZUP	Word puzzles.		Giving meanings.	Adjectives; jobs; colours; furniture.
14 How good is your memory?	Lists; notes; paragraphs.	Past tense.	Describing people and actions.	Action verbs; physical appearance.
15 Postcards	Lists; postcards.	Present tenses; past tenses.	Describing; giving opinions.	Describing people, places, weather, food.
16 School	Questionnaires; charts; paragraphs.	Questions; past simple; present simple.	Asking for information; speculating.	School subjects; school systems.
17 A pair of shoes	Labelling; sentences; paragraphs.	Present simple; would.	Describing people; speculating.	Clothes; physical appearance; personality.
18 Customs and traditions	Notes; sentences; paragraphs.	Present simple.	Describing customs.	Customs and traditions; action verbs.
19 Test yourselves	Designing tests.	Word order; question form; present tenses.	Describing photographs.	Social situations; geographical descriptions; personal information.
20 A writing board game	Spelling lists.	Present continuous; past and future tenses.	Describing actions.	Objects; words; street scenes.

To Lita, Daniel and Fiona.
Thanks.

Acknowledgements

My thanks to Adrian Doff whose initial vision of the materials set the ball rolling and whose insightful comments led to many improvements.

Thanks also to Alison Baxter, Jeanne McCarten and Barbara Thomas at CUP for their patience and sound editorial judgement, without which there would simply be no book.

Also to the members of the 1989 Teaching of Writing Group at the University of Lancaster who made a number of useful comments on the pilot version of the materials and gave me many insights into the nature of the writing process.

We would like to thank the teachers at the following institutions, where *Writing 1* was piloted, for all their constructive suggestions without which the improvements in the book would not have been made.

Studio School of English, Cambridge; IUT – GEii, Cergy, France; Beatrice Schildknecht, Wedel/Holstein, Germany; Australian College of English, Bondi Junction; Foreign Language School, Crete, Greece; VHS Hanover, Germany; Klubschule Migros, Bern, Switzerland; British Council, Thessaloniki, Greece; Box Hill AMEC, Australia; International House, Lisbon, Portugal; Brunswick AMEC, Australia; ITC 'Sandro Botticelli', Rome, Italy; Istituto Tecnico Statale per il Turismo 'Marco Polo', Palermo, Italy; Cambridge Centre for Languages, Sawston Hall, Cambridge; Veronica Crosbie, Japan.

The authors and publishers are grateful to the following for permission to reproduce photographs:
Barnaby's Picture Library (p.6); J. Allan Cash (p.7d, p.9a, b, c, e, h, p.46 Costa del Sol and Morocco, p.48 London, Athens and Venice); Popperfoto (p.46 Swiss Alps, p.48 Sydney and Bangkok); Sally and Richard Greenhill (p.62).

The photographs on p.9 (d, f, g) and pp.51–3 were taken by Jeremy Pembrey.

Drawings by Peter Dennis, Chris Evans, Elizabeth Haines, Leslie Marshall, Clyde Pearson and Trevor Ridley. Artwork by Peter Ducker, Pavely Arts and Wenham Arts. Book design by Peter Ducker MSTD.

Introduction to students

Writing 1 contains lots of different activities to help you learn English. Some of these will help you with writing itself but most of them will help you learn English generally, through writing.

The book is full of choices. You can do the units in any order and you do not have to do everything in each unit. (The units at the beginning of the book are a little easier than the units at the end and, usually, the first activities in a unit are the easiest.) If you want to practise a particular thing, look at the *Map of the book* on pages iv–v. That will tell you which unit it is in.

There are answers for some of the exercises at the back of the book. Usually, these answers are only examples of what you *could* write and your own answers may be very different. Exercises with answers have a symbol, like this: ⚷

For many of the activities in this book, you have to work with someone. Sometimes you will write something as a pair or a small group and then give it to some other students. Sometimes you will write something by yourself and then compare it with your neighbour. The point of this is not just to write, but to talk about writing. In this way, you will improve not only your writing but your general knowledge of English as well.

We hope you learn a lot from this book and enjoy using it.

1 | Home sweet home

1 What do people do at home? Look at this picture. First write in the name of each room. Then add what we usually do there.

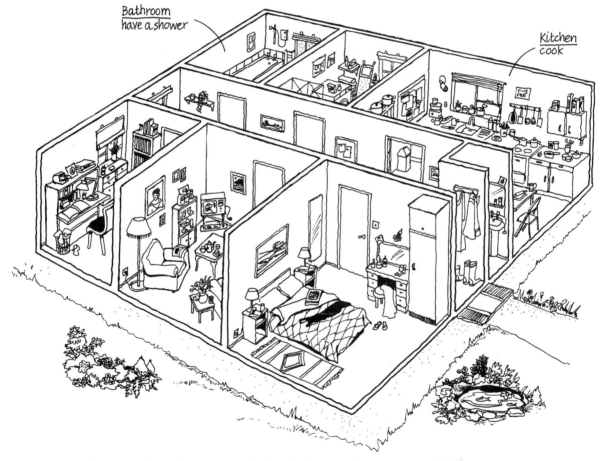

cook   read   sleep   wash the dishes   clean   watch TV
eat   wash clothes   have a shower   get dressed   relax
keep clothes   make coffee   drink coffee   iron   play ball games
study   play card games   wash

Can you think of any other things we do at home? Add them to the picture.

2 What do you like doing at home? What do you dislike doing at home?
Make three lists – one of things you like doing, one of things you dislike
doing and one of things you do not mind. Like this:

like	dislike	don't mind
watching TV	cleaning	cooking

Now think about another student in your class. What do you think he/she
likes, dislikes and does not mind? Write some sentences for him/her to read.

I think you like cooking.
I think you don't mind washing clothes.
I think you dislike playing ball games.

When you are ready, exchange papers. Were you right?

3 Home is . . . What makes a home? Home is important to people in different
ways. What title can you give to these pictures?

a)

Home is a nice cup of coffee.

b)

Home is watching TV.

c)

d)

e)

f)

g)

h)

What is home to you? Write some 'Home is . . .' sentences about what you
think. Read them out to the rest of the class.

4 Could you live in this house? What is wrong with it?

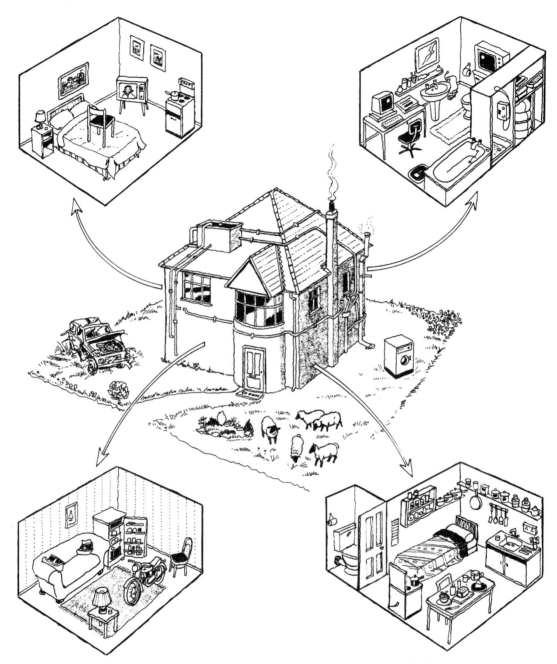

Write as many sentences as you can, saying what is wrong with the house.
Use a dictionary to help you. Here is an example:

There's a TV in the bathroom. It should be in the living room.

Compare what you have written with another student. Do you agree?

2 | Around the world

1 How well do you know the world? Can you write the names of these countries in the right place on the map? Also, match the languages with the right countries.

Brazil   The Netherlands   Mexico   Belgium   Germany
Saudi Arabia   China   New Zealand   Switzerland   Italy

English   Arabic   Chinese   French   Dutch   Spanish
German   Portuguese   Italian

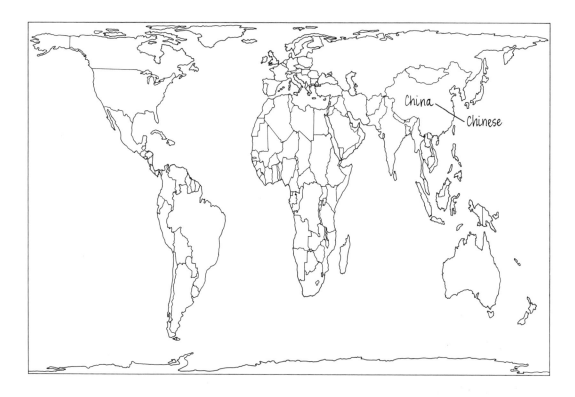

2 **Work in pairs. Think of five or six countries and write a sentence about each one like this:**

1. It's very hot there and they have a lot of oil.
2. They eat a lot of pasta there.

They eat . . .   They wear . . .   They speak . . .   They play . . .
They live in . . .   They have . . .   They . . .   It is . . . there.
There is . . .   There are . . .

You can write about any country, but here are some names:

Australia   Austria   Brazil   China   France   Greece
Ireland   Italy   Iceland   India   Japan   Saudi Arabia
Scotland   Switzerland   Spain   United States   Vatican City

When you are ready, give your sentences to another pair. They have to guess which countries you wrote about and say where they are on the map in exercise 1.

3 **Here are some places that people go on holiday. Why do you think they go there? Think of as many reasons as you can. Make some notes about each picture, like this:**

New York
to go shopping
to go to theatres

Use a dictionary to help you. Compare your reasons with other people in your class.

a) New York

b) The Swiss Alps

d) Safari Park, Kenya

c) Barbados

Here are some ideas:

to see beautiful scenery   to visit museums   to see famous buildings
to learn English   to enjoy good food   to take photographs

Why do people visit your country? Tell the rest of the class.

4 **Think of a country you do not know. Close your eyes and imagine you are there. What can you see? Make some notes, like this:**

Holland
- lots of bicycles
- very flat countryside
- fields of tulips

Choose one of these countries:

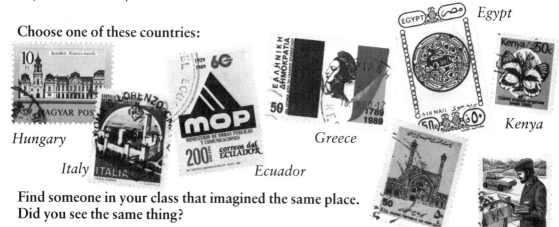

Hungary

Italy

Ecuador

Greece

Egypt

Kenya

Iran

Switzerland

Find someone in your class that imagined the same place. Did you see the same thing?

Is there anybody in your class who knows the country? Show your notes to them.

3 | Personal descriptions

1 **Look at this man.**
You can describe him
with just a few words.

– long, curly hair
– glasses
– round face

Now look at these people. Write a few words about two or three of them.
When you have finished, ask another student to match your description to
the right person.

beard
moustache
long/short/curly hair
fat
thin
tall
short
glasses
big/small/round nose
square/round/long face
big/small ears
happy/sad/serious

2 Write a few words about yourself on a piece of paper. Put everybody's descriptions together in a pile or envelope. Choose one and read it aloud. Who is it?

3 You can also describe people by saying what you think about them. Here are some words. What are the opposites?

beautiful   interesting   funny   nice   young   honest   rich

Look at the people below. What do you think about them?

a)

b)

c)

d)

e)

f)

g)

h)

9

Choose one or two of the people. Show what you think about each one.
If you can, say why. Make a chart, like this:

beautiful _very   quite   neither... nor...   quite   very_ ugly because he's got a big nose.

Show your chart to your neighbour. Does he/she agree? Why/why not?

4   You can use facts to describe a person, as well. Here are some sentences
about me, the author. Some of them are true and some of them are untrue.
Which sentences do you think are untrue?

1 I can speak more than five languages fluently.
2 I studied English at university.
3 I normally work as a butcher.
4 I work at Cambridge University.
5 I am married and have two children.
6 I live in a large house in the country.
7 When I wrote this book, I was about 50.

Now write some sentences about yourself, but make some of them untrue.
Give your sentences to another student to read. He/she has to guess which
are true and which are untrue.

4 | DOs and DON'Ts

1 Life is full of rules – things that we can and cannot do. What are the 'rules' for these situations? Work with a partner. Choose some situations and write some DOs and DON'Ts.

Talk quietly. Don't run or shout.

b) In a classroom

a) In a church, mosque, temple or synagogue

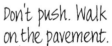

Don't push. Walk on the pavement.

c) Travelling on a train

d) In a cinema

e) In the street

Compare your ideas with others in your class. Do you all agree?

2

Often, there are notices to tell people what they can and cannot do. Where would you see these notices?

a) **_DO NOT WALK ON THE GRASS_**

b) **_PLEASE DO NOT FEED THE MONKEYS_**

c) **STAFF ONLY**

d) *Please take one*

e) **NO JEANS**

f) **_PLEASE QUEUE HERE_**

g) NO SMOKING AT THIS TABLE

What notices would you put in these situations? Work with a partner and write down your ideas.

a)

b)

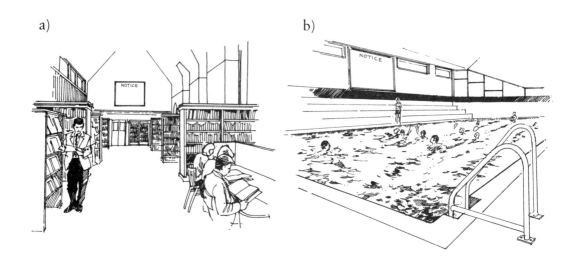

c)

d)

3

Many of the things that we do are very different in other countries. What do you do in your country when you:

- start and finish a meal?
- meet new people?
- meet male or female friends?
- leave people?
- answer the telephone?

Write about what you do in each situation. If you know what they do in another country you can also write that. For example:

In my country, we kiss when we meet friends.
In Britain, they just say 'Hello'.

When you are ready, tell the others in your class what you wrote. (There are some example sentences about Britain and other countries in the answer key.)

4

Some foreign friends of yours are going to visit your country. What advice would you give them? Write it down. For example, this is some advice about coming to Britain:

Learn some English before you go.
Drive carefully – on the left!
Don't use the telephone in the morning. It's very expensive.

Here are some ideas:

what to wear   money   learning your language   driving
eating   drinking   shops/restaurants   meeting people
places to go   places not to go   the weather

Exchange your papers with other students. If there are other people from your country in your class, do you all agree?

5 | Expectations

1 When you go to the doctor, what do you expect to find? Somebody like this?

Do you agree or disagree with these sentences?

1 He looks too dirty to be a doctor.
2 Doctors should have a tidy desk.
3 Doctors shouldn't put their feet on the desk.
4 Doctors normally shave.
5 Doctors don't normally play golf in the surgery.

What other things are wrong with the doctor in the picture?

2 Look at these pictures of a teacher and a pilot. What is wrong with them?

Write three or four sentences about each one. You can start:

- He/She looks too . . .
- He/She should . . .
- He/She shouldn't . . .
- Teachers/pilots normally . . .
- Teachers/pilots don't normally . . .

untidy   young   long hair   torn clothes   a magazine
slippers   a spelling mistake   smoke   shave

**When you have finished, compare what you have written with other people
in the class.**

3 We also expect things to be a certain way. What is wrong with these things? Write a sentence for each one. 🔑

a) The handle on the lid is missing.
b) One of the gloves has only got four fingers.

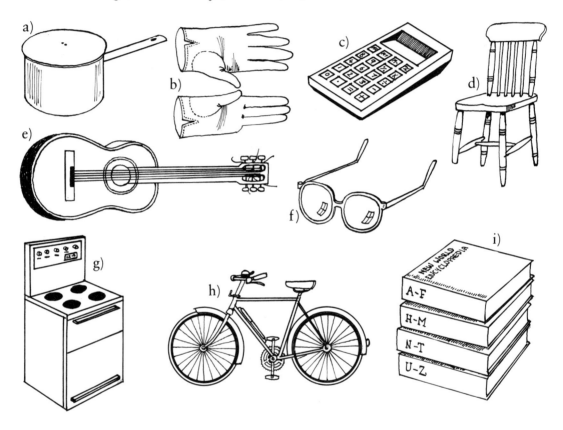

upwards   upside down   missing   too short   string   door
chain   finger   lid   arm   handle

4 Here is a description of a car. What is wrong with it?

Cars usually have four wheels, a motor and wings. they run on water and can go very fast. They taste very nice with tomato sauce but they are quite expensive to buy.

Work with a partner. Think of another thing and write a description of it. Make it wrong in some way and then give it to another pair in your class. They must tell you what is wrong.

6 | Help yourself!

1 What do you do in your English lessons? Work in a small group and make a
list of all the things you do, like this:

- Listen to the tape and answer questions.
- Read and answer questions.
- Dictations.

Which things do you think are most useful for you? Compare your ideas
with other groups' ideas.

How can you practise your English by yourself, outside the class? In your
group, make another list. These things might give you some ideas:

Try to think of some unusual ways to practise.
What ideas do the other groups in your class have?

2 One way to help yourself is to make your own practice exercises. Here are four types. Have you seen them before?

Gaps, e.g.

> *Fill in the missing word.*
> John is from Amsterdam. He's ....

Drills, e.g.

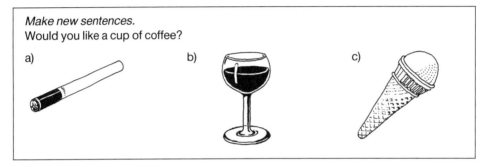

> *Make new sentences.*
> Would you like a cup of coffee?
> a)   b)   c)

Matching, e.g.

> *Match the opposites.*
> heavy   light   wide   quiet   ugly   expensive
>
> cheap   loud   light   beautiful   dark   narrow

Grammar, e.g.

> Put in the correct form of the verb.
> 1 John .... breakfast at 6.30 every day. (have)
> 2 Henry .... to the cinema last night. (go)
> 3 What does your father ....? (do)
> 4 I .... Helen yesterday. (see)

Look at your coursebook. Can you find examples of each type in your book?

Work in pairs. Write some exercises about your group. For example, you could write a matching exercise:

Pedro ⌐ is wearing glasses.
Mitsuko | smokes a pipe.
Helen └ speaks Spanish.

or a gaps exercise:

Jan is sitting _____ _____ Paula.
Stefan is _____ a _____ shirt.

or perhaps a drill:

Ingvar works in a bank.
1. Jaime/farm   3. Ella/travel agency
2. Kerstin/-   4. Terencio and Ernesto/factory

or maybe a grammar exercise:

1. We _____ here every week (come)
2. Peter _____ here last week (be, not)
3. _____ next week? (you, come)

When you are ready, give your exercises to another pair to do. (If you prefer, you can write exercises about something else – for example, your town or country, places, famous people, foods, jobs, or anything.).

3   **When you are learning English, it is useful to think about what you know. This can help you to see what you need to learn. Choose one or two situations from the list below and write down the things you can say there. Like this:**

(If you are not sure how to say something, write it in your language and try to find out before your next lesson.)

in a shop   in a restaurant   at a hotel   at a doctor's
at a railway/bus station   asking the way   meeting new people
meeting friends   talking about yourself   using the telephone

When you are ready, compare what you have written with your neighbour and with other people in your class.

7 | Business letters (1)

1 Can you complete this puzzle? Draw lines to show where each piece goes.

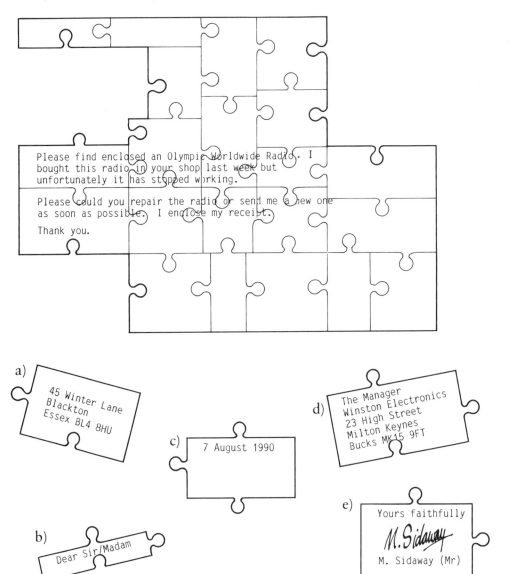

Please find enclosed an Olympic Worldwide Radio. I bought this radio in your shop last week but unfortunately it has stopped working.

Please could you repair the radio or send me a new one as soon as possible. I enclose my receipt.

Thank you.

a)
45 Winter Lane
Blackton
Essex BL4 8HU

b)
Dear Sir/Madam

c)
7 August 1990

d)
The Manager
Winston Electronics
23 High Street
Milton Keynes
Bucks MK15 9FT

e)
Yours faithfully

M. Sidaway

M. Sidaway (Mr)

Look back at your completed puzzle and then write five true sentences from this table.

The sender's address is	under the addressee's address.
The addressee's name and address is	at the end, on the left.
The date is	at the top, on the left.
'Dear . . .' is	under the sender's address.
The name of the writer is	at the top, on the right.

sender: The person who writes the letter.
addressee: The person who receives the letter.

2 How you close a letter depends on how you open it.

Dear Sir Dear Madam Dear Sir/Madam	Yours faithfully

Dear Mr Smith Dear Mrs Cheng Dear Ms Zayani	Yours sincerely

Dear Helen Dear Mohammed	Best wishes

Can you write in the missing openings and closings?

1 Ms W. Foster
   35 Mount Hill
   Woverton

   Dear ....
   Yours ....

2 Dear Marie
   ....

3 Ronco Beds Ltd
   67 Main Road
   Jacksonville

   ....
   ....

4 The Editor
   Daily News
   London

   ....
   ....

5 Dear Roger
   ....

6 The Manageress
   Pancho's Restaurant
   Buxton

   ....
   ....

3 Here are some more letters with parts missing. Write out each letter in full, using the phrases below. Also, add 'faithfully', 'sincerely' or 'best wishes'.

I am writing in connection with   Please could you
Please find enclosed   Thank you for your letter of

a)

```
                              26 Bowerham Rd
                              Lancaster
                              LA1 2BS
                              4 July 1990

     Minari Cameras
     Skeats Wharf
     Milton Keynes
     Bucks MK15 2NJ


     Dear Sir/Madam


     ------------------- your advert
     in The Times.
     ------------------- send me your
     new catalogue of Minari cameras.


     Yours -----------

              R.Ford

           R.T. Ford
```

b)

```
                              13 Green St
                              Edinburgh
                              EH2 8HT
                              8 May 1990

        British Telecom
        6 Sun Street
        Edinburgh


        Dear Sir/Madam


        ------------- 3 May.
        ------------- a cheque
        for my telephone bill.

        Yours -------------

          Alexander McKay

        Alexander McKay
```

c)

```
     Iberian Holidays Ltd
     67 Chester Rd
     London WC1


     Dear Mrs Williams


     ---------------------- send me
     your brochure and price list
     for holiday villas in Spain.


     Yours -----------

        Roger Cook

     Roger Cook
```

Now write short letters for each of these. Each letter should have two sentences. Lay them out correctly (see the letters on page 22 and in exercise 1 for examples).

a)   THE DAILY NEWS   7 January 1990

> # WANTED
>
> Salespeople to work from home.
> Earn up to £1,000 a week.
> No experience required.
> Application forms and details from:
>
> Mrs S. Spencer
> Brown Ltd
> 52 High Street
> Cornworthy
> Devon TR1 2TT

**Say why you are writing.
Ask for the forms.**

b)

THOMPSON'S GARAGE	26 Nelson Road Grange, Yorks GR3 6HJ

INVOICE NO. **297**   Date **6 March**

repairs to car   £280·76

Thank them for the invoice. Enclose the cheque.

c)

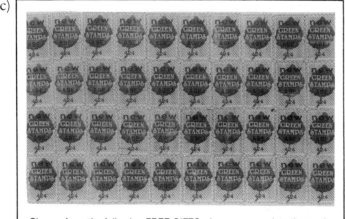

Choose from the following FREE GIFTS when you complete the card:

1. a pocket radio/cassette   2. an electronic toaster
3. a waterproof watch
Send to: Green Stamps Ltd, 67 Harrison Rd, Burnley BN3 4RJ, Lancs.

**Enclose the stamp card.
Ask for the gift you want.**

8 | On the road

1 In many countries, road signs are the same. Triangular signs warn you about something:

Be careful! Children cross the road here.

Red circular signs mean you must not do something:

You must not turn right.

What do you think these signs mean? Write a sentence for each one.

a)  b)  c)

d) 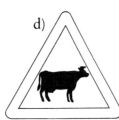 e)  f)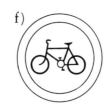

These signs are a bit strange. What do you think they mean? Write a sentence for each one. Then compare with your neighbour.

Draw some more triangular and circular signs of your own. Then give them to another student. He/she has to guess what they mean.

2   Here are some street directions. Can you match them to the correct map?

1   Take the second road on the right.
2   Take the second road on the left.
3   Go straight down the road until you come to the traffic lights. Turn right.
4   Go straight down the road until you come to the school. Turn right.
5   Turn right. The house is on the left.
6   Turn left. The house is on the right.

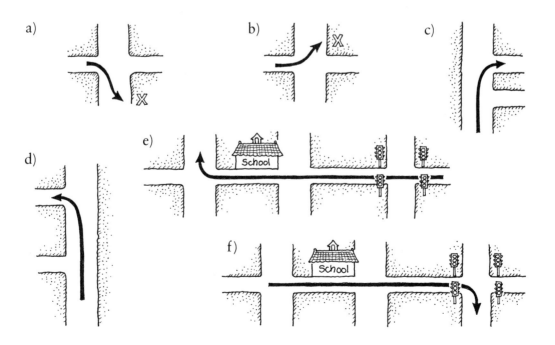

Here are some more directions. Where am I going? To A, B, C, D, E or F?

Go straight down the road and turn right. Continue until you come to the traffic lights. Turn left and then turn right. It is on the right.

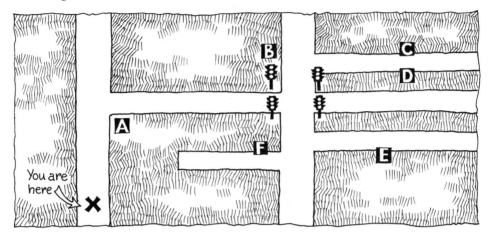

Now you try it. Choose two places on the map and write instructions to get there. Give your instructions to your neighbour. Can he/she find the way?

3   Travel is not always easy. What are these travel problems?

a flood   a traffic jam   a crash   a strong wind   fog   snow
ice   roadworks

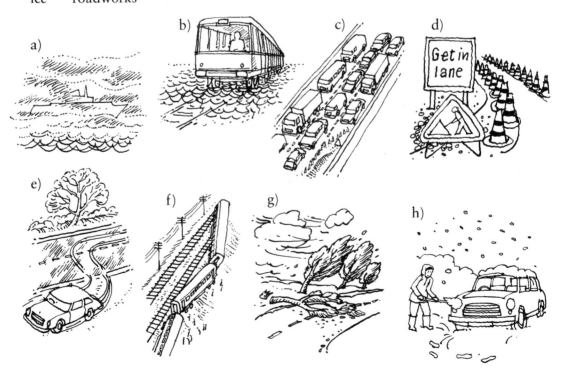

Look at the picture below.

Work in two pairs, pair A and pair B.

Pair A want to get from Blomberg to Torp. Make a list of all the possible ways to get to Torp. Try to use a different verb for each sentence. Like this:

We can fly by helicopter.

Pair B has to make a list of travel problems, like this:

There is fog. The helicopters can't fly.

You have five minutes. You can use a dictionary to help you. When the time is finished, exchange lists. Can pair A get to Torp?

9 | Forms

1 Look at these forms. Which form do you fill in if you want to:

– come into the United Kingdom?
– buy some furniture?
– start life insurance?
– go on a holiday?

LANDING CARD
Immigration Act 1971

Please complete clearly in BLOCK CAPITALS *Por favor completar claramente en MAYUSCULAS*
Veuillez remplir lisiblement en LETTRES MAJUSCULES Bitte deutlich in DRUCKSCHRIFT ausfullen

Family name
Nom de famille
Apellidos
Familienname

Sex
Sexe
Sexo **(M.F)**
Geschlecht

Forenames
Prenoms
Nombre(s) de Pila
Vornamen

Place of birth
Lieu de naissance
Lugar de nacimiento
Geburtsort

Date of birth Day   Month   Year
Date de naissance
Fecha de nacimiento
Geburtsdatum

Occupation
Profession
Profesion
Beruf

Nationality
Nationalite
Nacionalidad

Staatsangehorigkeit

Address in United Kingdom
Adresse en Royaume Uni
Direccion en el Reino Unido
Adresse im Vereinigten Konigreich

RA 951 100

Signature
Firma

Para uso oficial / Nur fur den Dienstgebrauch
POL

---

1 SURNAME (State Mr., Mrs., Ms., Miss)

2 FORENAME(S)

3 ADDRESS

POSTCODE

4 SINGLE ☐ MARRIED ☐ WIDOWED ☐
DIVORCED ☐ SEPARATED ☐ (Please tick)

5 DATE OF BIRTH

MALE ☐ FEMALE ☐ (Please tick)

6 HEIGHT: **7** WEIGHT:

8 OCCUPATION (Please describe fully)

Please tick 'YES' or 'NO' to these questions and sign and date the declaration.

A Do you engage in any hazardous activity or occupation (e.g. aviation, working at heights, climbing, diving, motor sports, etc.)?

B Have you ever had a serious illness or operation or are you now receiving any treatment or expecting any medical consultations, operations, treatment, blood or other tests or investigations as an in-patient or out-patient at any hospital or clinic or have you done ... five years?

YES   NO
☐   ☐

DECLA...
and I c...
informa...
attended...
physical...
from any...
been mad...
such infor...
answers to...
are true to t...

9 SIGNAT...

SPK
FURNITURE
BY POST
0792-33542

SPK *0792-33542*
SPK Designs, Ltd., P.O. Box 84, Swansea, SA2 3TF.

Please send me the SPK Catalogue.
I enclose a cheque/postal order for £1.95 made payable to SPK Designs Ltd.

Name ....

Address ....

.... *Post Code* *OB8*

MOROCCO
EVERYTHING YOU'D EXPECT.
MORE THAN YOU'D DREAM.

Please send me details of Holidays in Morocco   ST/90/2

Name _____

Address _____

_____

Moroccan National Tourist Office. 205 Regent Street. London W1R 7DE

Here are some words from the forms. Find each one on the form and then match it to the correct meaning.

1	address	a)	your job
2	signature	b)	LIKE THIS
3	place of birth	c)	where you were born
4	date of birth	d)	your family name
5	male/female	e)	your first names
6	occupation	f)	where you live normally
7	block capitals	g)	man/woman
8	forenames	h)	your personal way to write your name
9	surname	i)	when you were born

2

Here is some information about a man called Jim Foster. How would he fill in the life insurance form in exercise 1? Write his answers to points 1 to 8.

Jim Foster is married and has two children, Neil and Alison. He lives at 27 Mill Road, Manchester MR3 6TH and works as a teacher in a primary school. His birthday is on 15 July and he is now 50 years old. He is about 1 metre 70 cm. tall and weighs about 80 kilos.

What about you? How would you complete the life insurance form? Write your answers to 1–8.

3

Here is another form, but this time the name of each piece of information is missing. Can you write it in? Use block capitals!

Findafriend Agency

Romance and marriage can be for you! Fill in the form.

1. [   ] : WILLIAMS
2. [   ] : HENRY
3. [   ] : 16 HAMPTON ROAD
              BRISTOL BS6 2TX
4. [   ] : MALE   5. [   ] : 1 m 85 cms
6. [   ] : 87 kgs   7. [   ] : 16 JUNE 54
8. [   ] : TAXI DRIVER
9. [   ] : FISHING, READING AND PLAYING THE GUITAR
10. single ⊠   married ☐   divorced ☐   widowed ☐
11. [   ] : Henry Williams 12. [   ] : 13 SEPT 1990

---

4 Sometimes bureaucrats ask for information that they do not need. Look at the forms below. Do you think any of the questions are unnecessary?

a)

Snoworld Skiing Holidays Ltd

BOOKING FORM

Name: _____   Weight: _____
Address: _____   Colour of eyes: _____
Telephone No.: _____   Shoe size: _____
Date of birth: _____   Number of adults in group: _____
Holiday No.: _____   Number of children in group: _____
Date of holiday: _____

b)

SPECIAL OFFER!

Please tick (✓) which jumper you require.

	medium	small	large
blue squares	....	....	....
green squares	....	....	....
blue stripes	....	....	....
green stripes	....	....	....

name: ....
address: ....
....
.... postcode:.................

sex: ....   date of birth: ....
occupation: ....
weight: ....   I enclose a cheque for £ ....

Work in pairs. Can you make up a form for one of these people?

1 Someone who has lost a suitcase at a railway station.
2 Someone who wants to study English at your school.
3 Someone who wants to be a teacher in your school.
4 Someone who wants to join a sports club.
5 Someone who wants to find a penfriend.

If you want, put in some unnecessary questions!

Exchange forms with another pair and fill them in. Do you think any of the questions are unnecessary?

10 | Family life

1 Can you find the names of ten family relationships in this square? The words go across or down.

```
I  S  R  T  N  D  R  S  O  N
D  H  R  S  T  A  U  N  T  E
A  N  E  I  E  N  G  E  U  R
U  D  C  S  Q  W  S  O  N  R
G  F  A  T  H  E  R  E  C  E
H  G  M  E  R  S  D  H  L  V
T  B  V  R  T  S  C  N  E  W
E  B  R  O  T  H  E  R  G  I
R  Y  Q  I  P  O  I  T  E  F
T  Y  O  G  K  I  N  R  E  E
A  N  H  U  S  B  A  N  D  O
M  O  T  H  E  R  I  T  E  T
```

2 How many brothers and sisters do you have? How many aunts and uncles? Draw your family tree. Write a sentence about some of the people in your family. Like this:

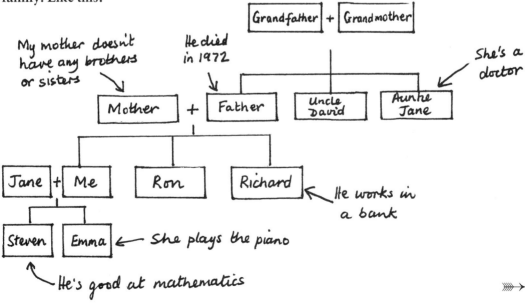

Exchange family trees with other students in your class. Find someone whose family is the same as yours in some way.
Tell the rest of the class what you find:

'I've got one brother and three sisters and so has Ahmed.'
'My brother lives in Germany and so does Anne's brother.'

3 **Read this passage about the Browns. As you read, complete the family tree below. Write something about each person.**

The Browns are a very strange family. Mrs Brown does not talk to her husband, Mr Brown, because he is rude to her. Mr Brown does not talk to his daughter, Norma, because she smokes cigars. Norma does not talk to her brother, Roger, because he bites his nails. Roger does not talk to his other sister, Gladys, because she eats meat. Gladys does not talk to her other brother, David, because he plays loud pop music. David does not talk to his mother because she does not like his girlfriend. Mrs Brown will not talk to Gladys and Norma because they have strange boyfriends. Roger and David do not talk to their father because he will not let them use the car.

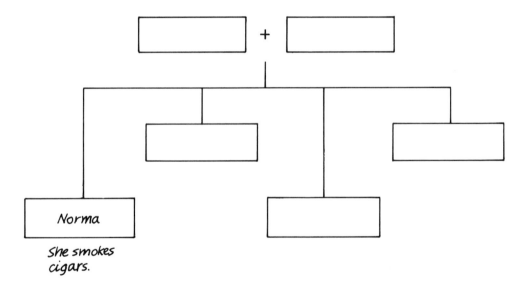

If Mrs Brown wants to tell Mr Brown something, how does she do it?

First she tells Roger. Roger tells . . .

4 **What should people in a family do? What shouldn't they do? What should they be able to do? Write down your ideas about some of the people below.**

mothers   fathers   husbands   wives   children   grandfathers
grandmothers   mothers-in-law   fathers-in-law

Like this:

Children shouldn't go to bed late.
Mothers should be able to go out to work.

Here are some ideas:

Who should do the housework?   cook the food?   go out to work?
   look after the children?   choose the children's friends?   choose
   a husband for a daughter?   choose a wife for a son?
When should children go to bed?   Should they get pocket money?
Should they do homework?

**Read your sentences out to the class or show them to your neighbour.
Do you all agree?**

11 | Business letters (2)

1 Read these letters. Which letters go together?

a)

Dear Sir/Madam

Six months ago we sent you 200 C60 cassettes. Unfortunately, we have not received your payment. Please could you send us a cheque for £175 as soon as possible.

Yours faithfully

b)

Dear Sir/Madam

Last week, I bought a pair of shoes from your shop.

Unfortunately, when I got home, I found that there was only one shoe in the box (Sunset model, size 7, left shoe). Please could you send me the other shoe as soon as possible.

Yours faithfully

c)

Dear Sir/Madam

Last month, I ordered two boxes of white paper from you. The paper has now arrived but, unfortunately, it is green not white. Please could you send me the correct colour as soon as possible. I am sending the green paper back to you today.

Yours faithfully

d)

Dear Mr Jackson

Thank you for your letter of 9 July.

I am sorry that we sent you the wrong colour paper. I am sending you two boxes of white paper today.

With apologies

Yours sincerely

G. F. Robertson

G. F. Robertson
Sales

e)

Dear Mrs Carrillo

Thank you for your letter of 12 July.

I am sorry that our payment for the cassettes is so late. I enclose a cheque for £175.

Yours sincerely

L. Turnstall

L. Turnstall
Manager

f)

Dear Mrs McEvoy

Thank you for your letter of 6 July.

I am sorry that there was only one shoe in the box. I am sending you the missing shoe immediately. I enclose a complete refund of your money.

With apologies

Yours sincerely

H. J. Norton

H.J. Norton
Manager

2

You bought the following things through the post. When you open them, this is what you find:

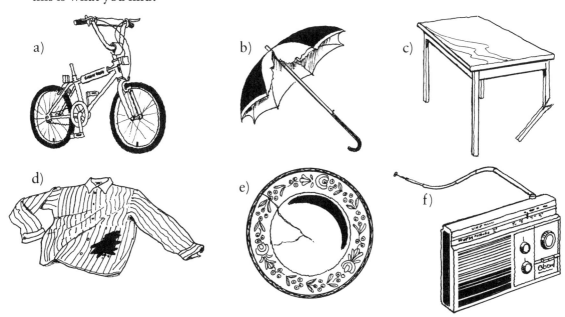

a)   b)   c)

d)   e)   f)

broken   torn   missing   stained   cracked   bent   upside down

Work in pairs. Choose an object and write a letter complaining, like this:

> *your address*
> *date*
>
> The Manager
> Thomson Catalogue Ltd
> 63 Bath Road
> Bristol BS5 7HK
>
> Dear Sir/Madam
>
> I have just received . . . from you.
>
> Unfortunately, + *the problem.*
> *Ask them to do something.*
>
> Yours faithfully
>
> *your signature*
> *your name*

(See Unit 7 for how to lay out a business letter.)

Give your letter to another pair. Write an answer to the letter that you receive. Like this:

Thomson Catalogue Ltd
63 Bath Road   Bristol BS5 7HK

date

name and address of the
person you are writing to

Dear (Mr/Mrs/Ms/etc.)

Thank you for . . .

I am very sorry that . . . *Say what you are doing about it.*

Yours sincerely

your signature
your name

---

3 Here are some letters. What is wrong with them? Can you make them sound better?

a)

HARVEST ELECTRONICS
43 Windermere Road, Torquay TQ1 5HH, Devon

Mrs B Davies   22 Sept 1990
124 Humbolt Ave
Torquay TQ1 3WS

Dear Madam

I am pleased to tell you that it
is not possible to repair your
Transworld EC900 radio. This
is because we cannot find the
new parts. Please could you
collect the radio from our shop
as soon as possible.

Yours faithfully

R P Jones

R P Jones

---

b)

CATON SCHOOL
8 Shaftesbury Road, Gillingham, Dorset

Ms J Winston
67 Station Road   16 Sept 1990
Manchester MR8 4RS

Dear Ms Winston

I am sorry to tell you that your
application for the post as teacher
was successful. I enclose a contract.
Please could you sign it and return
it as soon as possible.

We look forward to seeing you on
September 10th.

Yours sincerely

T. H. Hunt

T H Hunt
Head Teacher

---

c)

```
CRUNCHY BREAKFAST CEREALS LTD
          North Road
       London EC3 5TH

Mrs R Norden            5 Oct 1990
5 China Street
Lancaster
Lancs LA1 4YT

Dear Mrs Norden

I am sorry to tell you that you
have won the STAR PRIZE in our
competition. You will receive a
cheque for £1000 within the next
few days.

Yours sincerely

H R Windsor

H R Windsor
```

```
                    Hinley Properties Ltd
                    345 Kensington Avenue
                         Hinley HD4 8UH

                              3 October 1990
H Brown
4 Kings Road
Hinley HD6 8GF

Dear Sir/Madam

I am pleased to tell you that the
rent on your flat will rise from
£40 to £60 a week from 1st January
next year. This is because of the
rise in inflation.

Yours faithfully

N Smith

N Smith (Mrs)
```

d)

Are the following good or bad news? Write a letter about two of them.
Make up a reason, like this:

```
Dear . . .

I am pleased/sorry to tell you that . . .
This is because . . .

Yours . . .
```

1 The price of petrol will increase by 15 per cent next week.
2 We can raise your salary by 10 per cent next month.
3 We can offer you promotion to Head of Department next January.
4 Our factory will close down next year.

Show your letters to each other. Did you give the same reasons?

12 | Jobs

1 There are 12 names of jobs in this square. Can you find them? The words go from left to right or top to bottom.

```
E N G I N E E R W R
C L E A N E R A S O
A O I D Y T W R E T
R S D E G H M T C V
P O I N Y T Q I R D
W A I T E R X S E L
N D R I V E R T T A
T S C S B N V C A W
E B U T C H E R R Y
T E A C H E R W Y E
Q W S C D O C T O R
E H O U S E W I F E
```

2 Here is a list of jobs, activities and personal qualities. Write two sentences about each job. Choose the personal quality that you think is most important for each job.

Artists	build houses.
Police officers	repair teeth.
Librarians	help people to learn.
Teachers	look after the children and the home.
Bricklayers	paint pictures.
Dentists	choose and organise books.
Parents	read the news.
Radio announcers	try to find criminals.

They have to be	easy to understand.
	creative.
	quiet.
	patient.
	strong.
	gentle.
	good at everything.
	honest.

When you have finished, show your sentences to another student. Do you agree?

Do you have a job? What do you do in your work? What qualities do you need to have?

3 What do people work with? Write a sentence about five or six of the jobs in the list in exercise 2 or about any other jobs. Like this:

They use sand and cement and a trowel.

When you are ready, give your sentences to another student. He/she has to say which job each sentence is about.

4 What do you expect from 'good' dentists, teachers, nurses . . .? Work in pairs. Choose a job from the list and make some notes, like this:

<u>Good dentists</u>
– gentle
– find the problem and
  make it better
– explain what they're
  doing
– nice to talk to

dentists
actors
engineers
mathematicians
bankers
chefs
nurses
watchmakers
architects
writers

Then write a short paragraph, like this:

Good ? are gentle. They find the
problem and make it better. They always
explain what they're doing. They are
also nice to talk to.

Give your paragraph to another pair. They have to guess which profession you have written about.

5 Why do people work? Only for money? In pairs, make two lists.
One list should have all the *good* things about work. The other list should have all the *bad* things about work. Which list is the longer?

<u>good things</u>   <u>bad things</u>
you get money   you have to get up early

13 | DROW SELZZUP*

1 Work with a partner. Choose a puzzle and try to do it. Then check your answers in the answer key.

a)

Find the names of eight colours.

A	S	O	R	A	N	G	E	R	T
W	H	I	T	E	U	I	O	P	G
Z	X	C	V	B	N	M	L	K	R
Q	W	E	R	L	G	H	J	U	E
A	S	X	C	U	J	K	B	O	Y
L	K	P	I	E	H	G	L	R	D
D	C	V	G	B	H	N	A	M	K
G	R	E	E	N	O	L	C	J	R
M	N	H	Y	G	F	V	K	E	E
U	Y	E	L	L	O	W	S	D	D

b)

Fill in the names of jobs.
What word do they make?

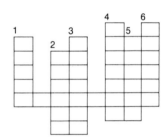

Someone who . . . 1) looks after you in hospital. 2) sings songs. 3) looks after your teeth. 4) helps you learn. 5) brings you food in a restaurant. 6) gives you medicine.

c)

Match the halves of words together to make the names of eight pieces of furniture.

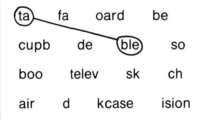

ta   fa   oard   be

cupb   de   ble   so

boo   telev   sk   ch

air   d   kcase   ision

d)

Here are the names of eight fruits.
What are they?

GERONA   PELPA   REPA

GERPA   MONEL   CATOPRI

ANABAN   HECAP

*Word puzzles

40

In pairs, try to make another puzzle like the one you just did. You can make your puzzle about the name of anything, but here are some ideas:

fruit   vegetables   foods   drinks   furniture
plants   things in the room   verbs   adjectives

Write the answers on the back of the paper. When you are ready, give your puzzle to another pair for them to do.

2   Here is another type of word puzzle. How many sensible sentences can you make with the words in this box? You have two minutes. (You can use each word more than once.)

smoking	green	girl	that	small
brother	have	I	is	years
car	a	there	are	people
ten	my	here	no	old

Now make a word box of your own. Like this:

— First write down four or five sentences with five or six words in each sentence.
— Count how many different words you have.
— Draw a box like the one above.
— Write in the words in any order.

See how many sentences you can make and then give your word box to another student to do.

3 **How good is your vocabulary? Choose the right meaning for each word below.**

1 to apologise   a) to clean
                        b) to say sorry
                        c) to talk loudly

2 pleasant   a) sad
                        b) nice
                        c) relaxing

3 a vase   a) something to eat
                        b) something to put flowers in
                        c) something to sit on

4 to snore   a) to cut wood
                        b) to run very fast
                        c) to make a noise when you are asleep

5 a drawer   a) something to put things in
                        b) a picture
                        c) something to write with

Now you make up a test. Find some 'difficult' words in your coursebook and write down three possible meanings for each one. (One of the meanings must be correct!) Give your wordlist to some other students to do.

4 **Here are two puzzles that you have to think about. Can you do them? Talk about them with your neighbour.**

1 A seven-year-old girl lives in a block of flats on the twelfth floor. Every day, she gets in the lift, goes down to the ground and walks to school. When she comes home, she gets in the lift, goes to the sixth floor and then walks up to the twelfth floor. Why?
2 Some boys are camping near a river. They want to make some soup. They need exactly six litres of water but they only have a nine-litre pot and a four-litre pot. How can they get six litres?

Do you know any puzzles like those? Make some notes about a puzzle and then try to write it down. When you are ready, put all your puzzles together. Take one and read it. Can you solve it?

14 | How good is your memory?

1 Mrs Brown went to the market because she wanted to buy . . . What did she want to buy? Make a list of ten things.

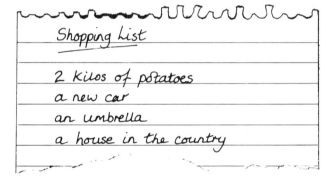

Shopping List

2 kilos of potatoes
a new car
an umbrella
a house in the country

Now exchange lists with a partner. Look at your partner's list for one minute and then give it back. Try to write down what was on the list. How many things can you remember?

2 Can you remember what you see? Look at the pictures on this page and the next page for one minute.

Now close the book and first, write down some notes describing the man.
Then, turn to page 75.

3 What about actions? Can you remember what happens? One person in your
class should do some actions, slowly. The others have to watch him/her and
then write down what happened like this:

First she touched her head. Then she walked
to the door and yawned. After that she turned
round and said 'Hello'.

Here are some actions:

touch his/her head   walk to the door   sing   say . . .   write
stand up   read   yawn   turn round   sit down   close his/her eyes

When you are ready, check with the person who did the actions. Did you
remember everything?

4 Can you remember when you were a child? Think about a house you lived in when you were a child. What was it like? Make some notes, like this:

- a big garden
- three big bedrooms
- very cold in winter
- a black dog and two rabbits
- always full of people

Using your notes, tell the others in your class about your house.

What is the first thing you can remember? Write two or three sentences about it.

I can remember when I was five.
I started school and I cried a lot.
My teacher was a man. He was very fat.

I can remember when I was six and a half. I went to the beach with my mother. I was very happy because I found lots of crabs.

Read your memory out to the other students in your class. Who has the youngest memory?

15 | Postcards

1 When people go on holiday, they often write about the weather, the food, the place and the people there. How can you describe them? Make four lists with the words below (some words can go in more than one list).

Weather	Food	Place	People
cold	delicious		

cold   delicious   boring   friendly   hot   awful
exciting   rude   nice   interesting   spicy   rainy
windy   beautiful   helpful   warm

2 Here are some postcards. Use the sentences which follow to write a message for each card. Choose a beginning, a middle and an end.

The beginning:

a) *Dear everybody,*
We arrived safely in Switzerland.

b) *Dear Jim and Kathleen,*
Here we are on the beach!

c) *Dear Katie,*
Morocco is wonderful!

The middle:

d) *The weather is beautiful, the people are very friendly and the food is delicious. Yesterday, we went to a carpet market like the one in the picture.*

e) *It's terrible! It's very hot and there are thousands of people here. There's no place to sit. The food is awful.*

f) *The weather is fantastic, but unfortunately, I broke my leg skiing yesterday.*

The end:

g) *Home on Saturday – Thank goodness!*
Best wishes,
Ron

h) *I don't want to come home!*
Love
Alex XXX

i) *Now I can't walk and I have to stay in the hotel all day. It's very boring.*
Home on Thursday.
Love, Marie.

3 Here are some more postcards. Choose one and imagine you are there.
What can you write? Work with a partner and make some notes.
You can make notes about: – the people
– the food
– what you did/saw yesterday
– what has happened

Paris

Venice

Athens

London

Sydney

Bangkok

Using your notes, tell the others in the class what
you imagined. Did they imagine the same thing?

4 **Below are some famous characters. Have you heard of them? Which one do you think wrote this postcard?**

Dear all, I arrived here safely. It's very cold and windy but the mountains are really beautiful. Our food isn't very nice. We eat everything from packets and tins. Yesterday we put up our flag. Home soon, best wishes,

a) *Neil Armstrong, first person on the moon.*

b) *Florence Nightingale, famous nurse in the Crimean War.*

c) *Edmund Hillary, first person to climb Mount Everest.*

d) *Christopher Columbus in America.*

e) *Roald Amundsen, first person to reach the South Pole.*

Work in pairs. Choose one of the other characters. What do you think he/she saw? Write his/her postcard but do not sign it. (Or, if you prefer, write a postcard from some other person who is famous in your country.)

Look at the postcard above and exercises 1 and 2 for help. Look at the picture and use your imagination! You can write about:

     – the place, what you can see   – the people
     – the weather   – what you have done
     – the food

When you are ready, give your postcard to another pair. They have to guess who it is from.

16 | School

1 Which subjects did you do (or are you doing) at school? Make a list and then put them in order of how important you think they are. If you can, add a note about why you think each subject is useful/important. Like this:

1. English – useful for travel or work.
2. Mathematics
3. Geography
4. History
5. Chemistry

Here are the names of some more school subjects:

Economics   Biology   Physics   Religious knowledge
Physical education   Business studies   Art   Languages
Environmental studies   Botany   Sociology   Politics

Compare your list with other students in your class.

2 What was (or is) school like for you? Work in pairs and make up four or five questions about school. Like this:

1. What was/is your best subject at school?
   Why did/do you like it?
2. What was/is your worst subject at school?
   Why didn't/don't you like it?

You can make up questions about anything but here are some more ideas.

– sports?
– uniform?
– meals at school?
– punishment?
– games?
– friends?
– teachers?

When you are ready, ask another pair for their answers. Make a note of what they say and then tell the other people in your class what you found out.

3 When do people go to school in your country? What schools do they go to?
What examinations do they do? Make a chart like this:

<u>Education in England and Wales.</u>

19 _	University / Polytechnic	Teacher Training	Other colleges (eg, music, art, medical)
18 _			
17 _	Sixth form College	Further Education College	} 'A' levels
16 _			
15 _			G.C.S.E Exams
14 _	Secondary School.		At secondary school you learn a foreign language.
13 _			
12 ____			
11 _			
10 _			School usually starts at 9.00 am and finishes at about 3.30 pm, Monday to Friday.
9 _	Primary School		
8 _			
7 _			
6 _			
5 ____			
4 _			
3 _			
2 _			
1 _			

You can leave school at 16

You have to start school at 5

Compare your chart with your neighbour. How is your chart different from
the chart about England and Wales?

4 Below are some details about some real people. What do you think they were
good at at school? When did they leave school? Did they go to university?
What did they study? Write a few sentences about each person, like this:

Helen is 37. She is a mechanical engineer.

I think she was good at
mathematics at school.
I think she studied
engineering at university.

a) Jane is 40. She is a bilingual (Spanish–English) secretary. She works for a big London bank.

b) Peter is 42. He teaches English to adults in Sweden.

c) Emma is 28. She is a sculptor. She has made a lot of sculptures for famous people.

d) Neil is 30. He works in a bookshop as a sales assistant.

e) Sarah is 35.
   She is a dentist.

Compare what you have written with your neighbour. Then look in the answer key to see the truth.

17 | A pair of shoes

1 Look at the picture below. Can you write in the name of each item of clothing? Say if it is:

– patterned   – striped   **or** – checked

Compare with your neighbour and then look in the answer key.

2   Look around the classroom. What do people have on at the moment?
Choose a person and write about him or her, like this:

The person is wearing a red checked sweater, a white shirt
and a pair of light brown trousers. He is also wearing a
scarf. His shoes are brown. He doesn't have a tie on.

Read out your description to the rest of the class. Can they guess who the
person is?

3   Below are some situations. What would you wear? Write a sentence or two
about each one, like this:

1. I'd wear my dark blue suit, a white shirt, my tie and
my black shoes.

1   You are going to work.
2   You are going to a wedding.
3   You are going to an interview for a new job.
4   You are going on a long journey by train.
5   You are going to paint your house inside.
6   You are going to dinner at a friend's house.

Exchange sentences with your neighbour. Would you wear the same type of
clothes in each situation?
If your neighbour comes from a different country, find out if your clothes
would be suitable there.

4   Clothes can tell us a lot. Even one piece of clothing can say a lot about a
person. Look at the shoes on the next page. Imagine you can see a person
wearing one of the pairs. What sort of person is he/she? Make some notes
about what you can see. Use your dictionary to help you. Like this:

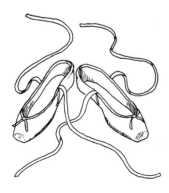

– a young girl
– long hair
– a pale face
– rich parents
– she's very quiet
– she can play the piano.

a) b) c) d) e) f)

Now use your notes to write a paragraph about the person you imagined. Give him or her a name. Like this:

Helen is a young girl. She's very thin and she has long hair. Her face is pale like the moon. Her parents are rich and she lives in a large house. She's a quiet girl and she doesn't talk very much. She can play the piano very well.

When you are ready, compare your paragraph with another student who wrote about the same shoes. Read your paragraphs out to the class.
Do you know anybody who wears shoes like the ones in the picture? What sort of person is he/she?

56

18 | Customs and traditions

1 **What is typical of your country? What is the national dish and drink, the national dress, the national game and the national working week? Make some notes, like these ones about Britain:**

National dish
Breakfast: bacon, eggs,
   tomato, sausage,
   toast.
Dinner: roast beef,
   Yorkshire pudding,
   peas, carrots, roast
   potatoes.

National game
Cricket
Football

National drink
Tea with milk
Beer at room temperature

National dress
There isn't one.

National working week
Monday to Friday,
9 to 5.
Lunch at 1 p.m.,
Dinner at 5.30.
Shopping on Saturday.
A drive or walk on Sunday.

If there are students from other countries in your class, compare what you have written. Ask each other about the things in your notes.

'What's a sari?' 'It's a long piece of cloth. Ladies put it around themselves like a dress.'

If there are other students from your country, see if you all agree.
Do many people eat, dress, drink, and live like that in your country?

2

Celebrations are very important in most countries. Below are some dates that people celebrate in Britain. Do you celebrate any of them in your country?

New Year's Day
Nobody goes to work.

Pancake Day
We eat lots of pancakes.

Easter
Children paint eggs.

January
1 2 3 4 5 6 7
8 9 10 11 12 13 14
15 16 17 18 19 20 21
22 23 24 25 26 27 28
29 30 31

February
1 2 3 4 5 6 7
8 9 10 11 12 13 14
15 16 17 18 19 20 21
22 23 24 25 26 27 28

March
1 2 3 4 5 6 7
8 9 10 11 12 13 14
15 16 17 18 19 20 21
22 23 24 25 26 27 28
29 30 31

April Fool's Day
People try to trick you.

April
1 2 3 4 5 6 7
8 9 10 11 12 13 14
15 16 17 18 19 20 21
22 23 24 25 26 27 28
29 30

May
1 2 3 4 5 6 7
8 9 10 11 12 13 14
15 16 17 18 19 20 21
22 23 24 25 26 27 28
29 30 31

June
1 2 3 4 5 6 7
8 9 10 11 12 13 14
15 16 17 18 19 20 21
22 23 24 25 26 27 28
29 30

May Day
Nobody goes to work.

July
1 2 3 4 5 6 7
8 9 10 11 12 13 14
15 16 17 18 19 20 21
22 23 24 25 26 27 28
29 30 31

August
1 2 3 4 5 6 7
8 9 10 11 12 13 14
15 16 17 18 19 20 21
22 23 24 25 26 27 28
29 30 31

September
1 2 3 4 5 6 7
8 9 10 11 12 13 14
15 16 17 18 19 20 21
22 23 24 25 26 27 28
29 30

October
1 2 3 4 5 6 7
8 9 10 11 12 13 14
15 16 17 18 19 20 21
22 23 24 25 26 27 28
29 30 31

November
1 2 3 4 5 6 7
8 9 10 11 12 13 14
15 16 17 18 19 20 21
22 23 24 25 26 27 28
29 30

December
1 2 3 4 5 6 7
8 9 10 11 12 13 14
15 16 17 18 19 20 21
22 23 24 25 26 27 28
29 30 31

Halloween
Children dress up as witches.

Guy Fawkes Day
People light fireworks.

New Year's Eve
People have parties. At midnight they sing a special song.

Christmas Day
We give each other presents.

Look at the calendar again. What other dates do you celebrate in your country? Make a list and write a sentence or two about each one.

When you are ready, exchange your list of dates with another student. Compare what you have written. Read out your list to the rest of the class.

3 Many other things are very different in different countries. What do you do in your country on the following occasions? Discuss one of them with others in your class.

a wedding   a wedding engagement   a child's birthday
an 18th or 21st birthday   a new baby   your Saint's Day
graduation from school/university   moving to a new house

Now choose one occasion and make some notes. Use your dictionary to help you but try to keep it simple. Like this:

Weddings in Britain
– only one day
– in a church
– a meal in a hotel or restaurant
– a party in the evening

(If you prefer, make some notes about some other occasion in your country.)

Using your notes, write a short paragraph. Like this:

In Britain, weddings usually take only one day. Many people get married in a church and, after the wedding, there is often a big meal in a hotel or a restaurant. In the evening, there is normally a party.

Find someone else in your class who wrote about the same thing. Compare your paragraphs. Read them out to the class.

19 | Test yourselves

1 Here is a test with four parts. Can you do it?
Write your answers.

TEST OF ENGLISH

PART 1
Fill in one word in each space.
Edinburgh is the capital city .... Scotland. About half a million .... live there.
The city .... very old and there are a .... of interesting buildings. Thousands
of tourists .... Edinburgh every year, especially .... August when there is a
festival. .... is a large castle on the hill above the city.

PART 2
Put the sentences in the right order.
a You're welcome.
b No, it's only about five minutes from here.
c Yes, you go straight down the road and turn left.
d Excuse me. Do you know where the nearest bank is?
e Is it far?
f Thank you.

PART 3
Put the words in the right order.
1 name Peter my is Smith.
2 200km I Bristol live from about London in , .
3 secretary an I office in as a work.
4 job like very I my much.

PART 4
Write down what you would say.
1 You want to know the time. You ask someone in the street.
2 You are on a train. You want to open the window. You ask a man opposite you if
   he minds.
3 You are at the bus station. You want to know the times of the buses to London.
4 You are in a restaurant. You want a glass of water.

60

2 Work with a partner. Make your own 'Test of English'. Look back at your coursebook and make a test with two or three parts. Look at exercise 1 for examples.

> **PART 1**
> *Fill in one word in each space.*

Write a paragraph or find one in your book.
Take out every sixth or seventh word.

> **PART 2**
> *Put the sentences in the right order.*

Write a dialogue or find one in your book. Mix up the sentences.

> **PART 3**
> *Put the words in the right order.*

Write some sentences or choose some from your book.
Mix up the words.

> **PART 4**
> *Write down what you would say.*

Think of some situations where you want to know or get to do something. They can be in the street, in a shop, in a restaurant, on a bus, in a railway station, on the telephone – anywhere.

Write the answers on the back of your test.

When you are ready, put all your tests together. Mix them up and then choose one. Can you do it? Remember to check your answers.

3 Look at this picture. In pairs, take it in turns to ask each other the questions below.

Where do you think these people are?
What do you think the woman is doing?
What is the boy doing?
How old do you think he is?
What do you think their house looks like?
What do you think they are going to do next?

Look through your coursebook. Find an interesting photograph and write down six or seven questions about it. When you are ready, interview your partner.

20 | A writing board game

How to play
for 2–6 players

You will need:
   a dice

a watch with a second hand

1   Put two books together, like this:

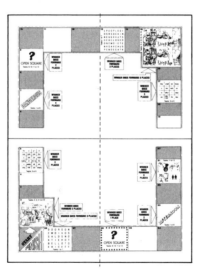

2   Everybody starts at square 1.

3   Each person throws the dice. If someone lands on a task square *everyone* must do the task.

4   The person who landed on the task square chooses the task.

5   You have one minute to do the task. YOU MUST WRITE YOUR ANSWERS. The winner is the person who has the longest/most answers. He or she moves forward the number of places shown.

6   The winner is the first person to land on FINISH.

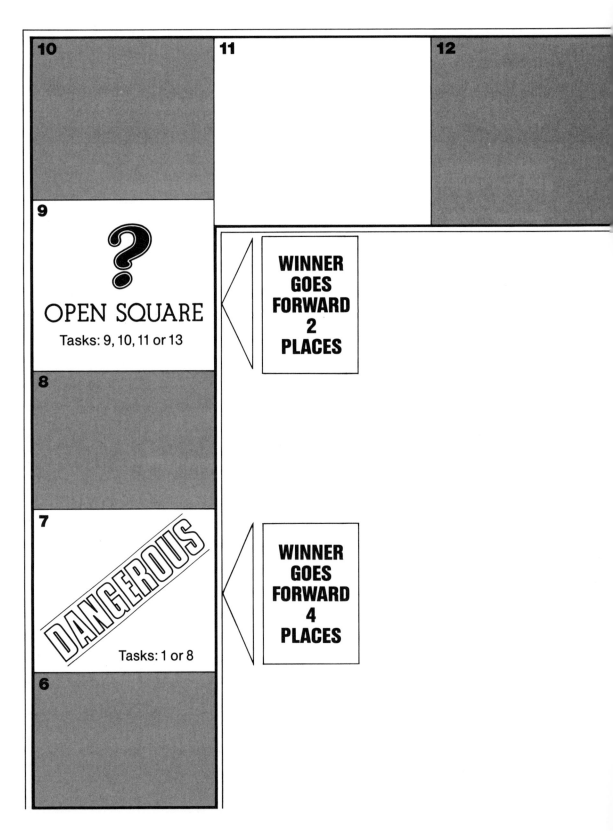

10

11

12

9

?

OPEN SQUARE

Tasks: 9, 10, 11 or 13

WINNER
GOES
FORWARD
2
PLACES

8

7

DANGEROUS

Tasks: 1 or 8

WINNER
GOES
FORWARD
4
PLACES

6

14

```
L P E O P L E S I
O S R S O C K I N
N E G G X V U T S
D E O C L O S E D
O N E M O I E T E
N V S A V C A U S
P E N D E E A T K
```

WINNER GOES
FORWARD
3 PLACES

WINNER GOES FORWARD 3 PLACES

WINNER
GOES
FORWARD
3
PLACES

15

Tasks: 3, 4, 12, 13, 14, 15

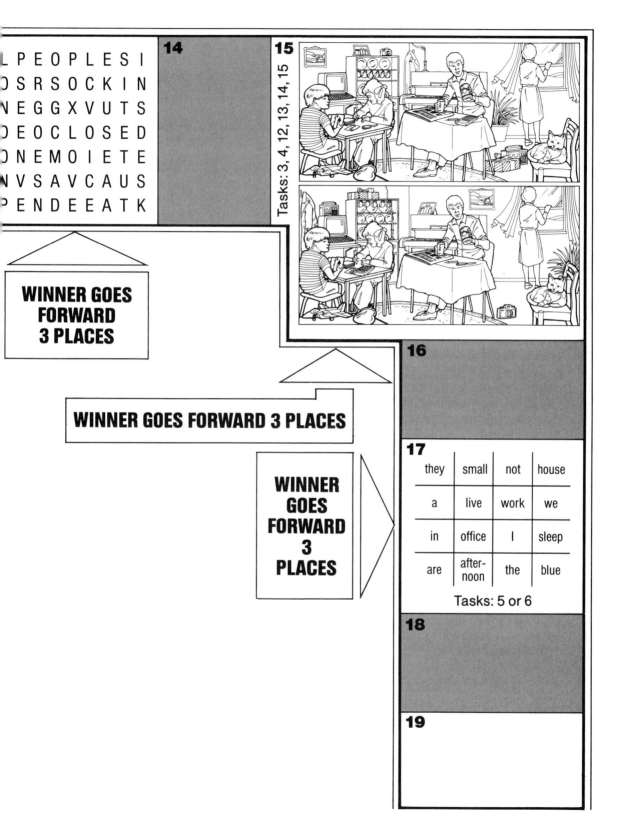

16

17

they	small	not	house
a	live	work	we
in	office	I	sleep
are	after-noon	the	blue

Tasks: 5 or 6

18

19

5

the	a	girl	in
was	book	coat	blue
a	and	car	made
reading	of	driving	the
is	leather	tall	and
song	little	sad	singing

Tasks: 5 or 6

WINNER GOES FORWARD 3 PLACES

TASKS

1 Make as many words of your own as possible with the letters.

2 Write down everything in the picture that begins with B or C.

3 Name as many things as possible in the picture.

4 Write as many sentences as possible about what is happening in the picture.

5 Make as long a sentence as possible.

6 Make as many different sentences as possible.

7 Find as many words as possible.

4

3

2   Tasks: 2, 3, 4, 5 or 12

WINNER GOES FORWARD 2 PLACES

WINNER GOES FORWARD 3 PLACE[S]

1

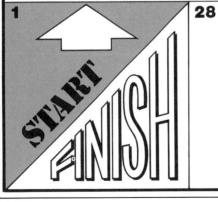

START
FINISH

28

D	O	O	R	S	O	N
E	W	D	I	X	O	S
S	A	L	D	S	N	O
K	T	I	E	H	O	T
B	E	L	L	O	T	O
E	R	I	C	E	E	E

Tasks: 1 or 7

27

8 Write as many different sensible sentences as possible using the word.

9 Name as many animals as possible.

10 Name as many things as possible in the room where you are.

11 Write down as many names as possible of . . . you decide!

12 Write a sentence in the past about the picture.

13 You decide!

14 Find as many differences as possible between the pictures.

15 Write down everything in the picture that begins with C or P.

20

21 Tasks: 11 or 13

22

WINNER GOES FORWARD 3 PLACES

23

AFTERNOON

Tasks: 1 or 8

WINNER GOES FORWARD 2 PLACES

WINNER GOES FORWARD 1 PLACE

25

?

OPEN SQUARE

Tasks: 9, 10, 11 or 13

24

Answer key 🔑

Unit 1   Home sweet home

1 **Possible answers:**

kitchen	*bathroom*	*bedroom*	*living room*
cook	get dressed	get dressed	read
clean	wash	sleep	watch TV
make coffee	have a shower	keep clothes	relax
drink coffee	wash clothes		play card games
eat			drink coffee
wash clothes			
wash the dishes			
iron			

study	*garden*	*wash room*
study	relax	wash clothes
read	play ball games	iron

3 **Possible answers:**

a) Home is a nice cup of coffee   b) Home is watching TV   c) Home is a warm bed
d) Home is a family   e) Home is lying in the bath   f) Home is relaxing in the garden
g) Home is a nice meal   h) Home is reading the paper.

4 **Possible answers:**

There is a TV in the bathroom. It should be in the living room.
There is a computer in the bathroom. It should be in the study.
There is a cooker in the bedroom. It should be in the kitchen.
There is a chair on the bed. It should be in the kitchen.
There is a washing machine in the garden. It should be in the kitchen.
There are some sheep in the garden. They should be in a field.
There is an old car in the garden. It should be in a rubbish dump.
There is a toilet near the kitchen. It should be somewhere else.
There is an electric socket near the sink. It should be somewhere else.
There is a bed in the kitchen. It should be in a bedroom.
There are pipes outside the house. They should be inside the house.
There are not any windows downstairs. There should be some.
There is a motorbike in the living room. It should be outside.
There is a refrigerator in the living room. It should be in the kitchen.

Unit 2 Around the world

1

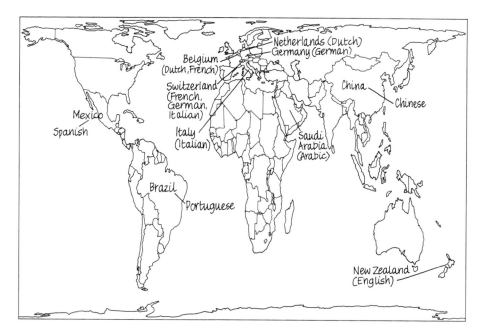

3 **Possible answers:**

a) *New York*
to go shopping
to go to the theatres
to visit museums
to enjoy good food
to see famous buildings
to learn English

b) *The Swiss Alps*
to get fresh air
to go walking
to get peace and quiet
to take photographs
to see beautiful scenery

c) *Barbados*
to go swimming
to sunbathe
to relax
to meet people

d) *Safari Park, Kenya*
to take photographs
to see wild animals
to see beautiful scenery

Unit 3 Personal descriptions

3 **Possible answers:**
beautiful–ugly; interesting–boring; funny–serious; nice–horrible;
young–old; honest–dishonest/crooked; rich–poor.

4   1 False.   I can speak English, Spanish (quite well), Swedish (quite well), and a
              little bit of French.
    2 False.   I studied Sociology and then Linguistics.
    3 False.   I teach at a university, I write and I study.
    4 False.   I work at Lancaster University.
    5 True!
    6 False.   I live in a small house in the town.
    7 False.   I was about 35.

Unit 4   DOs and DON'Ts

1   **Possible answers:**

a) Talk quietly. Don't run or shout. Sit still. Don't eat. Don't smoke.

b) Listen to everybody. Ask questions if you don't understand. Help the other students. Don't fall asleep.

c) Don't put your feet on the seats. Don't play loud music. Don't drop rubbish. Be calm and quiet.

d) Don't wear a hat. Don't eat loudly. Don't smoke. Watch the film. Sit still. Don't talk.

e) Don't push. Walk on the pavement. Don't drop rubbish.

2   **Possible answers:**

a) in a park   b) in a zoo   c) in a restaurant, shop, library, etc.   d) next to some information sheets   e) outside a restaurant, a bar or a club   f) somewhere where they sell tickets, e.g. a railway station or bus station, a theatre   g) in a restaurant

Possible answers:

a) Quiet please. / Silence. b) No running. / No jumping. / No ball games. / No flippers. c) Entrance. / Keep clear. / No parking. / Please do not park here. d) Please do not touch. / Quiet please.

3   **Possible answers:**

In Britain, they do not say anything when they are going to start a meal. In France, they say 'Bon appétit'.

In Britain, they do not say anything when they finish a meal. In Sweden, they say 'Tack för maten' (Thank you for the food).

In Britain, they shake hands when they meet new people. In Japan, they bow to each other.

In Britain, they say 'Hello' when they meet a friend. In Italy, they kiss each other.

In Britain, when they leave people they just say 'Goodbye'. In Mexico, they kiss each other.

In Britain, they say their number when they answer the telephone. In Sweden, they say their name.

Unit 5   Expectations

2   **Possible answers:**

a) He looks too untidy to be a teacher. Teachers do not normally make spelling mistakes. He should shave. Teachers do not normally have long hair. He shouldn't sit on the desk. Teachers do not normally eat while they are teaching. He shouldn't smoke in the classroom.

b) She looks too young to be a pilot. She shouldn't read when she is flying. Pilots do not normally wear slippers. She shouldn't put her feet on the controls. She shouldn't listen to music while she is flying. She shouldn't sleep while she is flying.

3   **Possible answers:**

a) The handle on the lid is missing. b) One glove has only got four fingers. c) It hasn't got a number '5'. d) One leg is too short. e) The guitar has only got five strings. f) The arms are upside down. g) The door opens upwards. h) The chain is missing. i) The letter 'G' is missing.

Unit 7   Business letters (1)

1   **Pieces like this:**

a
c

d
b
e

The sender's address is at the top, on the right.
The addressee's name and address is at the top, on the left.
The date is under the sender's address.
'Dear . . . ' is under the addressee's address.
The name of the writer is at the end on the left.

2   1 Dear Ms Foster; Yours sincerely
    2 Best wishes
    3 Dear Sir/Madam; Yours faithfully
    4 Dear Sir/Madam; Yours faithfully
    5 Best wishes
    6 Dear Madam; Yours faithfully

3   a) I am writing in connection with . . . ; Please could you . . . ; faithfully
    b) Thank you for your letter of . . . ; Please find enclosed . . . ; faithfully
    c) Please could you . . . ; sincerely

Possible letters:
a) Dear Mrs Spencer
   I am writing in connection with your advertisement for salespeople in The Daily
   News on 7 January.
   Please could you send me the application forms.
   Yours sincerely
   (name)

b) Dear Sir/Madam
   Thank you for your invoice of 6 March.
   Please find enclosed a cheque for £280.76.
   Yours faithfully
   (name)

c) Dear Sir/Madam
   Please find enclosed a stamp card.
   Please could you send me a . . .
   Yours faithfully
   (name)

Unit 8   On the road

1   a) You must not turn round on the road.
    b) Be careful! They are repairing the road.
    c) You must not go faster than 40 miles/kilometres an hour.
    d) Be careful! Cows are sometimes on the road.
    e) Be careful! Trains can cross the road.
    f) You must not ride a bicycle here.

Possible answers:
a) Be careful! Flying saucers/UFOs are in the area.
b) You must not sleep while you are driving.
c) You must not sing while you are driving.
d) Be careful! They sell fast food here.
e) You must not read while you are driving.
f) Be careful! Ghosts are in this area.

2   1–(c), 2–(d), 3–(f), 4–(e), 5–(a), 6–(b).
You are going to D.

Unit 9   Forms

1   1–(f), 2–(h), 3–(c), 4–(i), 5–(g), 6–(a), 7–(b), 8–(e), 9–(d).

2   1 FOSTER   2 JIM   3 27, MILL ROAD, MANCHESTER
POSTCODE: MR3 6TH   4 MARRIED   5 15.07.??   MALE
6 1m. 70cm.   7 80 kgs   8 PRIMARY SCHOOL TEACHER

3   **Possible answers:**
1 Surname   2 First names   3 Address   4 Sex   5 Height   6 Weight
7 Date of birth   8 Occupation   9 Interests   11 Signature   12 Date

4   a)   shoe size (?)
        date of birth (?)
        weight (?)
        colour of eyes
      b)   sex (?)
        occupation
        weight (?)
        date of birth

Unit 10   Family life

1

```
I S R T N D R(S O N)
(D)H R(S T(A U N T)E
A N E I E N G E(U)R
U D C(S)Q W S O(N)R
G(F A T H E R)E(C)E
H G M(E)R S D H(L)V
T B V(R)T S C N(E)(M)
E(B R O T H E R)G I
(R)Y Q I P O I T E(F)
T Y O G K I N R E(E)
A N(H U S B A N D)O
(M O T H E R)I T E T
```

3

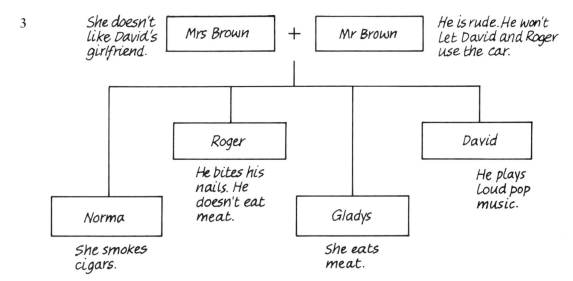

First she tells Roger. Roger tells David. David tells Norma. Norma tells Gladys. Gladys tells her father.

Unit 11 Business letters (2)

1   a–e, b–f, c–d.

2   **Possible answers:**
   a) I have just received a bicycle from you. Unfortunately, the seat is missing. Please could you send me one immediately.
   b) I have just received an umbrella from you. Unfortunately, it is very torn. Please could you send me another umbrella as soon as possible.
   c) I have just received a table from you. Unfortunately, one of the legs is broken. Please could you send me another table leg as soon as possible.
   d) I have just received a shirt from you. Unfortunately, it is stained. Please could you send me a new shirt as soon as possible.
   e) I have just received a plate from you. Unfortunately, it is cracked. Please could you send me another plate or send my money back.
   f) I have just received a radio from you. Unfortunately, the aerial is bent. Please could you send me a new radio as soon as possible.

3   Letters (a) and (d) should say 'I am sorry to tell you'.
   Letters (b) and (c) should say 'I am pleased to tell you'.

   1 I am sorry to tell you . . .
   2 I am pleased to tell you . . .
   3 I am pleased to tell you . . .
   4 I am sorry to tell you . . .

Unit 12   Jobs

1

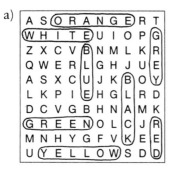

```
E N G I N E E R W R
C L E A N E R A S O
A O I D Y T W R E T
R S D E G H M T C V
P O I N Y T Q I R D
W A I T E R X S E L
N D R I V E R T T A
T S C S B N V C A W
E B U T C H E R R Y
T E A C H E R W Y E
Q W S C D O C T O R
E H O U S E W I F E
```

2   Artists paint pictures.
Police officers try to find criminals.
Librarians choose and organise books.
Teachers help people to learn.

Bricklayers build houses.
Dentists repair teeth.
Parents look after the children and the home.
Radio announcers read the news.

Unit 13   DROW SELZZUP

1   a)

```
A S O R A N G E R T
W H I T E U I O P G
Z X C V B N M L K R
Q W E R L G H J U E
A S X C U J K B O Y
L K P I E H G L R D
D C V G B H N A M K
G R E E N O L C J R
M N H Y G F V K E E
U Y E L L O W S D D
```

b)

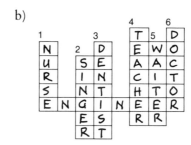

c)   table, sofa, bookcase, television, chair, bed, desk, cupboard.
d)   orange, apple, pear, grape, melon/lemon, apricot, banana, peach.

2   **Some examples:**
My brother is ten years old. That girl is smoking. My car is green. There are no people here. That small girl is smoking.

3   1b, 2b, 3b, 4c, 5a.

4   1   She was only seven years old and she was not very tall. She could not reach the button for the 12th floor.
2   They fill the nine-litre pot and then fill the four-litre pot from the nine-litre pot. That leaves five litres in the nine-litre pot. They pour the water out of the four-litre pot and fill it again from the nine-litre pot. That leaves one litre in the nine-litre pot. They pour the water out of the four-litre pot and pour the one litre into it. They fill the nine-litre pot again and then pour water into the four-litre pot until it is full. The four-litre pot needs three litres to be full so that leaves six litres in the nine-litre pot.

Unit 14   How good is your memory?

2   Which man was the thief?

Unit 15   Postcards

1   **Possible answers:**

Weather	*Food*	*Place*	*People*
cold	delicious	boring	cold
hot	cold	awful	boring
awful	hot	exciting	friendly
nice	awful	nice	rude
rainy	nice	interesting	nice
windy	spicy	beautiful	interesting
beautiful			beautiful
warm			helpful
			warm

2   a–f–i; c–d–h; b–e–g.

4   The postcard is from Edmund Hillary.
    Possible postcards from the other characters:
    a) *Neil Armstrong:* Dear all, I arrived here safely. It's very quiet and cold up here
       and there are no signs of life. I can see the Earth very clearly and it seems so far
       away. Yesterday, we walked on the moon for the first time. It was really difficult!
       Tomorrow, we will do some more experiments and we will return home. With
       best wishes, X.
    b) *Florence Nightingale:* Dear all, I arrived here safely after a long and tiring
       journey. The situation here is terrible. There are many sick and dying soldiers
       and we have no medicine or bandages. I have asked for some but they say that
       they will take many weeks to arrive. It is difficult to keep things clean. The men
       are dying from their wounds. I hope things will improve soon. With best wishes,
       X.
    d) *Christopher Columbus:* Dear all, I arrived here safely in India after a long, and
       difficult, trip. It's incredibly hot during the day but cool at night. The island that
       we are on is covered in dense jungle with many unusual plants. Tomorrow, we
       will make an expedition inland. With best wishes, X.

e) *Roald Amundsen:* Dear all, Here I am at the South Pole! There are no other flags here so I am sure I have reached the pole before Scott. We are all well and have no problems with food or our equipment. The weather has been terrible. All last week we had strong snow storms and we thought that Scott would get here first. Best wishes, X.

Unit 16   School

4   a) Jane wasn't good at anything at school. She left school at 16 and went to a secretarial college. When she was 20, she met a Spanish boy and they got married. She lived with him in Spain for three years but now they live in London.
b) Peter studied Mathematics at university and then he became a Mathematics teacher. A few years ago, he got married to a Swedish woman and went to live in Sweden. He cannot teach Mathematics in Sweden so he teaches English.
c) Emma has a Ph.D. in Botany. When she finished her Ph.D., she went to Art College for a year.
d) Neil was good at languages at school. He went to university to study English but he did not like it and he left.
e) Sarah was good at Physics and Biology at school. She went to a University Dental School.

Unit 17   A pair of shoes

1   a) a jacket
b) a checked shirt
c) a patterned tie
d) a checked sweater
e) a patterned dress
f) a blouse
g) a striped scarf
h) a striped shirt
i) a belt
j) a coat
k) a bra
l) a pair of pants
m) a pair of boots
n) a pair of patterned socks
o) a shoe
p) a pair of striped tights
q) a skirt

Unit 19   Test yourselves

1   *Part 1* of, people, is, lot, visit, in/during, There.
Part 2 d–c–e–b–f–a
Part 3 1 My name is Peter Smith. 2 I live in Bristol, about 200 km. from London. (other answers possible) 3 I work in an office as a secretary. 4 I like my job very much.
Part 4 (possible answers) 1 Excuse me, could you tell me the time, please? 2 Excuse me, is it OK if I open the window? 3 Could you tell me the times of buses to London, please? 4 Could I have a glass of water, please?

Unit 20   A writing board game

Square 2 Some things in the picture: cup, cigarette, car park, car, cinema, cabbage, carrots, caravan, cat, clock, coat, cloud, church, camera, ball, banana, bank, beard, bottle, bus, box, baby, bicycle, building, bag, bone, bird, butcher, boy.

Square 5 The longest sentence: The tall little girl in the blue coat made of leather is singing a sad song and reading a book.

Square 7 Some possible words: and, anger, are, danger, dog, gas, go, gun, nag, no, nod, our, ran, rang, red, rod, rode, run, sad, sand, sang, son, sun.

Square 13 Words in the square:

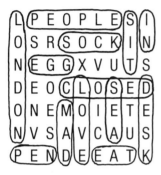

Square 15 Some things in the pictures: calculator, camera, can, candle, carpet, cassette recorder, cat, chairs, children, coat, computer, cupboard, cups, curtains, pen, pencil, penknife, photo, piano, picture, plane, plant, plate, present, purse.
The ten differences are:
The camera is now on the floor.
The present is now on the cupboard.
The cassette recorder is now on the computer.
The calculator is now on the children's table.
The photograph is now on the piano.
The candle is now on a shelf in the cupboard.
The picture is now above the piano.
The penknife is now on the man's table.
The coat is now next to the computer.
The plant is now on the other side of the window.

Square 17 The longest sentence: They are not in the small blue house.

Square 23 Some possible words: an, are, at, eat, fat, fate, net, no, none, nor, not, note, of, on, one, ran, rat, rate, rent, rot, tan, tar, ten, to, toe, ton.

Square 28 Words in the square:

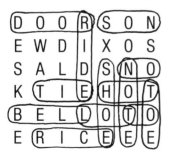

About *Writing 1*

Writing 1 is the first of four Writing books in the *Cambridge Skills for Fluency* series. The approach taken to writing in this and the next three books is possibly an unfamiliar one so you may find it useful to read the notes below which outline the basic principles behind the materials and give some general guidance for their use.*

1   Who is *Writing 1* for?

Writing 1 is intended for students with an elementary knowledge of English who may be studying in language institutes or in the upper classes of secondary schools.

2   What is the purpose of the book?

Writing 1 has two basic aims: firstly, to develop general language proficiency through writing; and, secondly, to develop the skill of writing itself. The first of these aims may seem unusual in 'skills' materials, so a word of explanation follows.

Writing, as a means of developing the students' general ability in English, is greatly undervalued in most language courses. Apart from the odd letter-writing task, general language courses usually restrict writing to tasks such as filling gaps, writing isolated sentences as part of a grammar exercise or doing a dictation. Yet there are a number of good reasons for bringing writing into a more central position in classroom work.

Firstly, in contrast to oral classroom work, writing can offer students the opportunity to work at their own pace and, above all, to think while they are producing language. Many students feel very anxious when they are called upon to speak in front of others and this anxiety effectively blocks their ability to think clearly. Handled correctly, writing can be less stressful. Secondly, writing can give students a chance to retrace their steps, to check and correct what they have written before they are required to show it to another person. This can allow more room for students to develop confidence in their language abilities, to develop their own understanding of

---

* For a fuller account of the rationale behind the book, see the article 'Learning to Write / Writing to Learn' by A. Littlejohn (publication forthcoming). The article won first prize in the 1989 English-Speaking Union English Language Competition.

78

how the language works and of what is 'linguistically possible'. Thirdly, unlike oral classroom work, writing can offer a permanent record; students can look back on what they have done, improve, check things, and refresh their memory of what they learnt in class. For these reasons, writing can offer students considerable opportunities to increase their vocabulary, to refine their knowledge of the grammar, to develop their understanding of how things are best expressed and how well their message is understood. In short, writing can offer more opportunities to learn.

In addition to the potential role of writing in general language development, however, there is also a 'skill' element to be considered – those abilities which are special to writing itself. There are at least four main aspects to this. Firstly, there is a knowledge of the different *types* of writing and the conventions of each (e.g. letters, postcards, messages, notices, reports, etc.). Secondly, there is an understanding of the *function* of a piece of writing and how that is accomplished: is it intended to amuse? to inform? to persuade? and so on. Thirdly, there is an understanding of the *structure* of a piece of writing: How is the text put together? Is there an introduction? How are examples given? How does the text end? and so on. Finally, there is the matter of the *process* of writing itself: what steps does the writer go through to produce a text? There are probably as many different ways to approach writing as there are writers, but some common ways one can identify are 'brain-storming' (jotting down points as they occur to you), making and organising notes, writing drafts, revising, writing spontaneously, dictating aloud to oneself and so on. As far as is relevant for students of General English at this level, the Writing books aim to develop each of these four aspects of writing. Through the Writing books as a whole, students are presented with many types of written text, are asked to consider their purpose and structure and are also introduced to numerous ways in which they can approach their own writing.

3   How is the book organised?

The book contains 20 units built around different topics. Each unit provides approximately 50–60 minutes of classroom work, although this may vary considerably from group to group and from student to student. The units can be done in any order but you will find that those towards the end of the book tend to demand more from the students. Within each unit, there are normally four or five different main activities. You can work straight through a unit from the first activity or, if you prefer, simply choose one or two activities as a supplement to your other work in class. Generally, the activities at the beginning of a unit concentrate on work at the level of vocabulary or phrases, whilst the activities towards the end demand sentence or paragraph writing.

4   What kind of activities does the book provide?

In fulfilling the first purpose of the Writing books – general language development – *Writing 1* aims to provide, as far as is possible at this level, open-ended, creative, imaginative tasks which will stimulate the students to use language to say what they wish to say and improve their fluency. You will find, therefore, few exercises with clearly right or wrong answers and few which require students to simply copy or produce 'parallel' texts. Many of the activities are interactive – that is, they require students to write to, for and with other students. The aim in doing this is to encourage the students to talk about writing and, thereby, learn from each other. Through working in groups to produce a piece of writing, students have an opportunity to ask each other – and the teacher if need be – about spelling, vocabulary, grammar, and the best ways of expressing things. Interactive writing tasks also give students a unique opportunity to get feedback from their readers on how far their message has been understood and, in so doing, fully integrate writing with the other three main skills – listening, speaking and reading.

As was mentioned above, the second purpose of the books, the development of writing skills, is accomplished by introducing various types of written texts (e.g. letters, postcards, notices), by asking students to consider the purpose of elements of a text, by identifying the structure of a text and by encouraging the students to try out different ways in which to approach their own writing. Most of these aspects, however, are not explicitly set out in the materials themselves, although the *Map* at the beginning of the book should enable you to locate a particular aspect of writing should you wish to do so. The aim has been to integrate the various aspects of writing as naturally as possible into the development of a particular topic so that students experience them as 'ways of working' rather than 'things to be learnt'.

Of the 20 units in the book, 13 deal with general topics, four deal exclusively with types of written texts (Units 7, 9, 11 and 15), and a further two deal with 'learning to learn' topics which encourage students to develop their own ways to help themselves learn (Units 6 and 19). A board game (Unit 20) concludes the book. The activities provided in the book range from the light-hearted to the more serious and it is hoped that teachers and students will be able to select units and activities which they find both interesting and useful to do. A concerted effort has been made to devise tasks which draw on the students' own experiences and opinions, thereby bringing about more involvement and placing teachers and students on a more equal footing.

5   How should the book be used?

As far as is possible at this level the instructions for each task are addressed directly to the students, making self-access use possible (an answer key is provided to enable students working alone to compare their own answers). Most teachers and students, however, will probably want to make use of the materials in class. It is hoped that the instructions for each task are clear enough to make further, detailed guidance for the teacher unnecessary but some general notes on the use of the materials may be useful.

If you are using the book to support your other classroom work, the *Map* at the beginning of the book will help you find a particular activity. The *Map* shows the main areas of language functions, language structure and vocabulary as well as an indication of the main aspects of writing covered in the units. If, however, you choose to do all the activities in a unit, you may find it useful to alternate between written work and oral work and, to this end, many of the activities will work just as well as a basis for discussion. The most important thing, though, is that when the students are asked to write, that they are given time to think, write, revise and discuss with their neighbours. With a class that contains students of varying levels of ability, this may mean that some students finish before others. A technique to reduce this problem is to 'chunk' tasks, that is, to ask students to do two or three before they return to whole class discussion. In this way, once students have finished a task, they can move straight on without waiting for others.

While students are writing, the teacher's job will mainly consist of circulating around the room. The key is for the teacher to be available and not to make the students feel defensive of their writing. Writing is unfortunately very commonly used as a means of evaluation so it is not surprising that many people feel they are being judged when they are asked to write something. If students do have problems in writing, some teachers find it productive to give hints or clues to the students rather than direct answers since this helps the students to develop the ability to write without assistance. It is worthwhile, for instance, keeping a few bilingual dictionaries and grammars available so that the students can check things for themselves, without having to ask the teacher all the time. Although this may appear to be time-wasting, it will help the students develop habits which they will almost certainly need when the course is over.

It is often quite useful to provide background music while the students are working. This could be classical music, jazz, blues – anything, although it is important to choose something that will not put anyone off. The mood of the music is also significant – if the writing activity involves two stages, one of a group/pair writing and the other of comparison with other groups/pairs, you might choose some calm, relaxing music for the first stage but something more energetic for the second stage.

Many of the activities in the book involve students working in pairs or small groups. It is usually best to set a time limit for group work, so that everybody knows how long they have on a particular task before they come together as a class. Since one of the main aims is to develop the students' understanding of how English operates, it does not matter too much whether the students discuss in English or – with a monolingual group – in their own language. In fact, an 'English only' rule, may make communication difficult and thus defeat one of the purposes of group work – to encourage students to help each other and share ideas. The most important thing is that what finally emerges is a piece of written English.

Some teachers may prefer to collect in written work for correction. One useful idea for this is to adopt a marking scheme. This involves putting a symbol in the margin indicating the kind of mistake that has been made (e.g. sp = spelling, w/w = wrong word, t = tense, w/m = word missing, w/o =

word order is wrong, w/f = wrong form (e.g. 'It were good'), ? = I don't understand!). This means that the students then have to discover for themselves what is wrong, and thus develop the ability to work independently of the teacher.

Writing 1 aims to provide a range of interesting and useful material which will enrich your language course. The tasks aim to bring about more personal involvement on the part of the students and give them the opportunity to use English to say what they wish to say. We hope that you enjoy using it.